1

I remember another time, a hand-me-down time,
a no-going-back time.
It was a time frozen in mid-step,
different from now; real.
Brown skinned, mostly naked kids; noise
and life.

Turquoise summer canopies,
hope and dreams wed to naivety;
a fervor born of youth and innocence,
an absence of vapor trails and hatred
and perfunctory ritual;
a time of laughter.

Innumerable yesterdays,
water under the bridge; no going back.
You can't go back, yet tomorrow never comes.
Today or nothing,
make do or do without;
cryptic nuance, logic.
God isn't kind, neither is nature.
Logic with a face; my face,
see?

A narrow, rutted, too-close country road;
cow trail.
I'd lay there for hours, staring, conjuring cars;
fulfilled, my stomach would leap!
Gasps and goosebumps, aii-ee!
Inexplicable, that dual sensation of fascination and
fear.
Hearing my mind shout, CAR!

I'd race for home, unseen flame consumed demons of
hell
closing fast upon my heels.

Hayseed; country bumpkin.
Damn right.
Goddamn right!
Proud of it.

Hot summer days and open prairie,
cowshit squished between bare, calloused toes
has never dried.
Gram used to scrub me in an old, battered wash tub.
"Wash behind your ears."
"Yes, grandma."
Grandma died in '56; maybe it was '57.
Hell, I wasn't there,
I was in town. Drunk.
"Stay away from the road", grandma used to say;
"Them city folks like to snatch kids."
"Okay grandma."
Later, I'd sneak down to watch for cars.

A man and woman stopped one day, offering candy.
They asked me to get into their car.
I ran like the wind, never looking back.
Gram never knew. I never again watched by the road.
I grew up, grandma, years after you left us.
You wouldn't like the way things are nowadays.
The old country road has four lanes.
Remember the old home place;
the window openings with no glass,
the ragged blankets that covered the doorway in
winter,
and carrying water from the creek?
God, how I miss those years.

The whole world has gone to hell, grandma.
Love is a dirty word.
It's hard to tell which way is north;
even the cowshit smells bad.
Joy and pain and tears and smiles;
what does it all mean?
Everything ends up at the same place.
We labor for nothing but to better pass the time;
aliens, the children emerge from nowhere
seeking already, the trails end.
Imagined gains and losses, in the final analysis are
neither.

Somewhere back in time every day was its own
answer,
now each presents an object lesson in absurdity.
Questions, questions,
Questions.
Truth somehow seems obscene, answers are relics.
Remember the rain, how it used to smell
even before it arrived, the subtle variance of nature's
voice,
red sky, warm wind, leaves turned upward;
remember then?
Now it's the stench of degradation.
We suffer the pasty sickness
of a time in which we have no place.

The sky is neither clear nor blue,
tears that fall from out the clouds
are noxious and acidic.
Nations decay for want of leaders,
leaders rot for want of followers,
neighbors curse and steal and whisper,
families exist in name alone;

the abomination of corruption, denied
is concurrently multiplied.
Fools are, fools do, fools, fools.
Cerebral drama, dreams of a distant time,
Visions;
grandma's voice calling.
Solace found in memories of childhood;
journeys of the mind.

Too much water under the bridge,
bullshit and truth and logic
and tears.
Junkyard automobiles, rust, shattered windows,
shapeless tombs, the burial place of dreams,
comfort to the homeless derelict, home;
where the heart is.
Not here; no, not here!

The dream returns, a vision lost, life.
Wine-muddied eyes behold a shimmering horizon,
new moccasins brush softly through sweet prairie
grasses,
lodge poles cradle an open sky; home.
Smiling, sun-bleached skin coverings,
the smell of charred meat from an open fire.
Spiraling slowly overhead
a copper-hued hawk screams and dives;
a distant time, a better place.
Dreams, visions,
Lies.

The stench of depravity struggles in snot-choked
nostrils.
Bottles' necks protrude from wrinkled, brown paper
sheaths,
the hunter reaches for an arrow,

reaches, reaches.
Blocking out the sun, a bottle tilted skyward
shares its final lie.
Again the hawk screams and dives,
eyes, again search the horizon.

Welcomed were you who came from the east;
damn you, damn you!
Goddamn you!
Like the plague of grasshoppers you came
and came and came.
Raven and coyote survive; how is it we do not?
Poisoned and hunted, coyote's numbers increase,
raven laughs in the face of genocide
yet do the People perish.

You offered the sanctuary of drink, salvation in a
bottle.
The People do not withdraw from encroachment
as does the grizzly,
instead we perish. Damn you and your kind!
Young girls giggle at your pubic brashness,
shiny trinkets bind their souls.
Awakened, the wild rose yawns,
glistening pink petals wither
beneath your contaminated stickiness.

The hawk screams and dives,
the long-tailed jumping mouse has failed to see.
Truth and death. Terminal education;
reality learned, too late.

Grandma sits quietly, braiding her hair;
the hawk screams and dives.
A time for crying, for smiling;
a time for remembering,

a time for
going home.

Like mountain thunder far to the west, the boisterous
wake of your passing scattered broken petals of youth
along the ridgeline of my heart, a few clinging
tenaciously on the edge of hope.

No more a sweet perfume of flowers wafting o'er the
meadows green, carried upward then on sky-bound
breezes, where heaven's angels wait in vain to bottle
paradise.

Art thou truly gone away my heart, in traveling robe of
velvet dream, seeking solace where none has lived?

I ask forgiveness, yet know full well that you must
continue on. Perhaps someday we'll meet again,
there I shall fall down on my knees to cry and beg
and whisper, please, forgive me.

Bridges span time's chasm, where spirits crossed at
will, entering a realm known to all who came and went
their ways, long before the world was born..
Bridges rusted, then collapsed, fallen into the oblivion
of eons knew the footfall of multitudes who trod this
fragile shoreline.
Recent arrivals, we who now ply life's tumultuous
waters are dysfunctional souls, encased within walls
of a vortex, a whirling maelstrom.
How many, the years that remain, how long this

drought of sanity?
Freedom pilfered, bits at a time; great emancipation of
lies.
Thus, upon a ragged talus slope,we fall, unchecked,
sliding down, and ever downward.

He'd never been to sea, yet he cast his words like a
fisher's net, the weighted skirts settling heavily over
her heart.
With a deft snap of his lip the cord strained, pulling
her stomach into a knot.
Old times were better, she thought, recalling kinder
words spoken.
He'd written them for her; the pretty rhymes,
and she used to recite them for all who would listen;

"On the far side, beyond side of Strawberry Ridge,
where the moon shadows hunker and whine,
the harsh wind of truth bid farewell to its youth;
to the trail of the sugary pine…"

He pulled the cord tighter;
"Goddammit, Jackie! I'm talking to you!"
She wished he wasn't.
The aurora was beautiful at this time of year,
and she was able to stand outside for long minutes
without really shivering from the cold.

"So wondrous, the first time your heart tasted
sunshine, how sweet, when those honey-lips smiled,
what treachery lurks in the mouth of deceit,

so often the poor fool beguiled..."

The door slammed (it already had, in her mind),
and she felt, more than heard the hollowness of his
leaving. Odd, she thought, how a grimmace can
resemble a smile. She wiped at her cheek. Why
couldn't she teach her eyes to lie?

"Wrapped in the nectar of wine-flavored comforters,
held by love's heady perfume, exposed to the hunter,
the heart of his prey,
no quarter, yet blind to its doom..."

Maybe, she thought, maybe even back then
the verses that now formed upon her mind's tongue
had been flowery harbingers crying for recognition.

" Oh sweet heart, dear face, your pure angel voice,
the sponsor of jelly-filled lies, how ghastly the
darkness that torments your soul, that seeks even
now, your demise."

She didn't hear the telephone ringing. The northern
lights had faded. Chocolate chip cookies!
Maybe she'd bake some cookies.....

Three steps right of center,
circulating, percolating, bubbling,
exuding enthusiasm and vigor,
a wild child in love with life.
I am reminded of the west wind
howling through ravines,
screaming over the Rockies,

tumbling across the Cascades.
The west is home, and to know
those remaining secluded places
where wild yet exists
and where we of the wild
are the kinfolk of freedom
is an honor given due respect.

Sweet scent of woman
Fills my soul
Skin, smooth and warm
Incites a tingling
Throughout my body

Hopeless, helpless man
Infatuated by her
And she smiles
Knowing I am trapped
By her charms

Germinated, sprouted, birthed of sorrow's seed;
sunlight smothered, moon deceased, ghetto newborn
baptized in oil of black decay.

Redneck cropper walks his barren fields, children
hang on mother's empty breast.

Mill worker laid off, home foreclosed, behind on
payments, car repossessed.

Fat cats flourish in penthouse suites, caviar and
lobster swilled with fine wines;

America, land of the free, home of the brave.

"…My Country, 'tis of thee…"

If other dimensions in time exist
why was it that I didn't find you
in a parallel galaxy
on a lush tropical island
long ago when we were young
taking our first childish steps
when love was a word believed
and sorrow had not been learned
could we but find our way back
crossing over that invisible bridge
perhaps this time we would meet
discovering our oneness
our bodies melding in harmony
in mind and in spirit
joined together forever

Scale then these craggy heights, while away thy
youth my friend, conscience damned and cast aside.
All that thou knew be trodden down, scoured by
frenzied fiends of time to be whipped of wind blown
sand.

Away, away to the earth's far end, seeking wisdom
the sages forgot, pilfered, plundered, purloined, lost,
gone as the careless blink of an eye.
Sold for the coin, tarnished and bent, in quest of elixir,
never relent.

Surly impediments to transition, remnants of
yesterday clutter and condemn as old news revived
stares balefully through windows.

Shards litter the floor, shattered secrets and
memories better forgotten emerge from corner and
crevice, whispered innuendo their forte.

Sleeping dogs awaken growling, the subtle warning
unheeded, another remembrance of love forsaken,
another day of tears recalling when you held my hand
for one brief moment, and then you said goodbye.

Cruel in its intensity, a chill wind howls, scouring
sand and sage; obliterating summer's sanity.

Gone, the warmth of yesterday's solstice, when sol-
splashed landscapes reigned, smiling upon picnics
and parades.

Nurtured by winds of October, the land stands stark
and bare, cold drizzle dampening fallen leaves,
pendulous gray clouds threatening.

Time now for reflection, smiling in remembrance of
spring's bright wardrobe while contemplating her
return.

Beyond my reach,
bearing no olive branch,
reality, borne upon wings of steel
screams across the universe
trailing flames of destruction.

Surely the good die young,
kicked from life's ladder,
the pinnacle never realized.

Shunned by righteousness,
veracity too late learns
of reality's harsh truths;
fortune smiling upon the wicked,
goodness shunned and despised.

Into murky pits of brimstone,
down in the muck of the lost,
cries drowned in the howl of icy winds,
faces ever forgotten,
bitter, the end at last revealed.

Sometimes in the quiet of an evening while enjoying the campfire's glow,
I take in all of the beauty and wonder of my mountain paradise and know without doubt that I am truly wealthy.

If afforded the option of anything beyond that which I possess I would decline the offer, for I have it all. There are times I wonder what shall be my lot should age and infirmity place me
in the unmerciful grip of circumstance, yet these fears are short lived, for as certain musical lyrics of old state, "surely goodness and mercy shall follow me all the days of my life and I shall dwell in the house of the Lord forever."

Hues of soft desert rose
filtered through curdled skies
play rainbow tunes
upon the desert sands

shades of purple crawl slowly
ascending massive cactus trunks
as the distant mesa becomes one
with a dark evening sky

a lone coyote's shrill yapping
intended for its brethren
happily finds my ears

my smile comes naturally

whether or not a creator
made this place where I stand
is unimportant at the moment
enough that it exists

Beyond the porch and up a gentle rise,
The woods open upon a small meadow.

Watching the cottontails playing here
Is a gift welcomed of the spirit's heart,
The young ones frolicking as young do;
Leaping, running, fur garbed amusers.

Deer foraging for acorns, alongside elk,
Are in abundance in this hidden place,
And here, wild turkeys feed without fear.

Giant ponderosa pines whisper softly,
Tickled by gentle mountain breezes;
The oaks, cloaked now in fall's red robe
Lend cheery splendor to the hillside scene.

Tranquility owns this secluded paradise,
We being simply appreciative guests,
Observing nature in her own home;
Thankful for the opportunity to be here.

The very best moments in life seem often to appear out of nowhere; radiant smiles that tickle the heart, tiny glimpses of good things to come; a bride's announcement of wedding bells, telephone calls from long lost friends, soft, cuddly puppies, given as gifts and issues resolved, with an end to life's rifts.

Huddled against morning's chill, early sun reflecting warmth from the weathered adobe wall, several Indians stir restlessly.

A night of drunkenness behind, indigent nomads awaken to begin anew, an endless quest, liquor the hunted quarry.

Pathetic souls, succumbed, victims of reservation life, torn between two worlds, between hogan and high rise, no longer welcome in either, drifting aimlessly, oblivious, children of another time.....
born too late.

Grandma sewed with needle and thread
by lamplight when we had kerosene
and handmade wax candles other times
her eyes growing dim over the years

she hand stitched clothing and quilts

repairing torn trousers and stockings
fabricating dresses and shirts and curtains
her work-worn fingers calloused and bent

She fought the old cast iron hand pump
priming and pumping, priming and pumping
until cool water rose up from the well
filling every type of container available

Feeding, herding and milking the cows
gathering eggs and slopping the hogs
harvesting vegetables from the garden
making butter in the old wooden churn

Always caring for her family; appreciating life
I suspect that even at this very moment
she is sitting with needle and thread
making little repairs to the wings of angels

Swift, the raven flies at night, feathers black as
pitchblende barely discernable against an indigo sky
where stars have perished and the moon faltered.

burden of torment be the message delivered upon ill-
conceived winds, bearing scent of burned sage and
oil of eucalyptus.

flee now before the dawn, when robin's breast be
crimson of its precious blood, spilled in violent
manner.

Away, be gone o' hoards of hell, permit the weary
timely demise, final cries extinguished, forever.

Covet not thy beauty, lovely one
For as the rainbow it must fade
And every joyous song was sung
Shall fall to ears which cannot hear

Love life, yea, and court not death
Still, to this single creed be true
Of all things in the universe
Not one be greatest; not one least

Observe all beauty while ye may
Which lieth everywhere about
Remember kindness in thy deeds
To help the weak and needy souls

Do good unto each that thou meet
Forsaking envy; turning from greed
A song of angels be thy challenge
To sing along in heaven's harmony

And when thy epilogue be penned
In book of life, oh loyal servant
Knowest thou, thy just reward awaits
Then go and claim thy prize with dignit.

Apple, offered with a smile.

Not just any apple,
the apple!
Sunlight splashed across bare thighs,
firm breasts lifted skyward;
Eve!
Adam's Eve; wanton, child-like,
whispering sweet promises,
wares peddled openly.
The lurking serpent strikes,
ecstasy embraced in garden grand;
moans amid ripe plum trees
heavy laden of sugary fruit.
Act completed, the damage done;
man evermore a willing slave.

Born in places high and free,
bubbling brooks care not a whit
for civilized convention,
nor of what fine gentlemen may think,
or lovely ladies, clutching skirts;
hurrying on their busy way.

Wild brook trout in frothy bath,
dance on tails amid the foam;
leap to where the hatch now hangs,
breakfast waiting in the air.

Soft deer nostrils test the scene,
tongues lick water, sweet and pure;
speckled fawn bleats softly
from ferns along the grassy bank.

A sacred place of ancient birth,

above a valley, never trod;
herein the idyll sought of old,
yet rests unfound, this paradise;
here rests unfound, God's own backyard.

Yesterday's promise gone, put out with the cat last
night.
Alleyway spats and yowling beneath the glow of
harvest moon, crickets in concert on garbage can
row.

Where goes the best of better days, the fresh,
unblemished face of love, whisked away to God-
knows-where, lost amid rubble of two hearts dissent.

Go then, upon divided pathways, the twain irreversibly
severed, seeking solace in the bottle's lie, purchasing
yet another promise,fleeting; temporary; deceitful.

Blind answers arrived
born upon frigid wings
as deaf ears slumbered
in hollow logs
and dilapidated houses

bones disintegrate
as heavy equipment
sits idle
and sanity
shrugs its shoulders

the mind gone still
all function ceased
birds without wings
feathers with no birds

tar pits beckon
boneless fingers extended
in final welcome

Oh, heart of my heart, soul of my soul, wonder of my
life, surely thou art sustenance, the bread of my
essence.
Thy beauty shines forth as though spires of sunlight,
saturating, radiating, illuminating all in thy presence.
Come hither, that I might touch thee, being then
blessed, consecrated through thy perfect holiness.
No love has been before thee, nor ever after shall
come, for nothing of earth may rival that which is
grace, that which is wonder, thee, my one true love.

God is not kind, nor is summertime, when midday heat devours the crop.
Hide ye spirits, beneath the bloom where scantest shade portends salvation.
Water become gaseous, rising fast away, parched lips crying out the more in vain.
Songbirds plummet from noxious clouds, a final sweet trill reaching stone-deaf ears, 'bringing in the sheaves' echoes endlessly, every goodness has gone astray, running amok.
As shadows scurry beneath their own, seeking anonymity's safe haven, crevices yawn amid crumbling pathways.

Condemnation of our species comes easily for the misanthrope. Observations of the human animal in its daily activities affords ample opportunity for finding fault. The mind of the newborn is predisposed to follow the path of least resistance in its social behavior. We enter this world with a penchant for good, evil, or myriad decisions affecting our lives and the lives of every person with whom we come into contact. Neither children or adults are taught the basic things of the mind. Nobody 'learns' to be homosexual, or to pursue a life of crime, yet do we delight in placing the blame for our attitudes and behavior on someone other than ourselves, seldom imagining that we were in fact born into our personal heaven or hell. And so, as the serial killer must kill, so must the poet write poetry; as the seasons are bound to change, so is the mind of the poet bound to write.

Thus it is that we walk our particular pathways, each of us locked into the ruts there.

The inside of time like a capsule from hades
sporting the whiskers of age and infirmity
oozing blood blacker than night of no stars
bats born of hell from brimstone suspended
demons nursing terror spawned offspring
curled in corners with serpents all hissing
reels now the image etched deep on the mind

undulating hips of seductress named death
lips form a scream with the very last breath
never the morrow shall raise up its head
every good thing on the planet be dead

Exploiters of the hungry heart, platinum coated
tongues aglow, these tickle ears all too willing,
feeding the spirit's malnutrition
on poisoned promises.

Sorrowful souls writhe in anguish, bodies undulating,
minds afire, salvation wrongly sensed.

Devils and demons thrive, utilizing wit, charm and deceit to entrap the gullible.

Tales recalled of a different time,
A time of make-do fishing poles,
When bare feet pattered in dust
On a hot summer day
Stories remembered of youth
On a faraway planet of dreams
Before vapor trails in the sky
When imagination was king...
Memories tucked neatly away
Languishing now and evermore
In albums of minds grown tired...
Tales recalled, stories untold
Carried away on spirit wings
Where time anew awaits

Prophets on the threshold of time,
place flowers at the feet of eternity,
yesterday's sanctions rescinded
as flame consumed wheels rotate
amid grotesque cumulonimbus.

Where gone, the youth of hope,
replaced with disparaging lies,

concealed within bleak admonition.

In silence, find thy way home,
seeking solace on a lost highway.

Time is ageless, for age exists only in the thoughts of men whose minds have dwelled too long upon the finite, upon things with beginning, and with end.

Show me an end, and I will tell you of a new beginning to that which you say ended; that which goes around comes around again.

In this universe (not unique) each is one and the one is all, where life entwines with life, and windows to yesterday reflect upon tomorrow.

Accepted theory, like an air-filled balloon, needs only the pin of things disbelieved and imagination scorned, to POP!

To hold your hand, to be your star,
to not distract from who you are;
To honor, love and offer strength,
forever, should life reach that length;
Your mate in sorrow, hardship too,
my soul and spirit offered you;
To start each day in your embrace,

at bedtime kiss your lovely face,
stand by your side, be never daunted,
my love, that's all I ever wanted.

Not tortured gasp, repentant vow or healer's caring
hand shall stay the rounds of unbiased death, or long
delay the nonselective cause of time, the soft and
sure decay of moral fiber, blood and bone, of all
things living, all things dead.

Windows in time , soiled and dirty, obstacles of
recall, detriment to memory, blurred images beckon.
Who are they? What do they want?
Windows in time sealed shut, nails rusted and
immovable.
Figures dance in and out of focus, windows through
time fly open upon a void.
Everything is gone, everyone vanished and I alone
remain.

Beneath, below, beyond that place of wildest
imaginings fly the spirits of another time.

Across a great abyss unseen by mortal eyes a
multitude of souls disenfranchised by life as known to
the living weep without end.

Excavate thee thy grave to be, while yet adequate
strength may be found in the supple sinew of youth.

She calls at night you know, and often in the voice of
things unknown, brittle sounds as though of scattered
ancient shards.
If dreams thou dream in restless slumber, bar thy
door and shutters then secure. When mist from out
the nearby swamp appears and filters through yon
transom cracks, pray thou breathe not the fetid vapor.
Should but the slightest odor waft into thy nostrils
friend, thy dream shall stop, and life then end.

Caviar for the fortunate few
Pork and beans for the poor
Potatoes and gravy and promises
A draft coming under the door

Run quickly, the tax man cometh
demanding thy last thin dime
Incentives proffered the wealthy
Whose lives know only sublime

Vote for the one who will save thee
With the smile and fine gilded lies
Believe all the rhetoric spoken
As thy bedridden progeny dies

Corruption and greed as a savior
The way of a people long lost
To hell with those at the bottom
Succeed, whatever the cost

A world just for you, that you prosper
To a neighbor, turn your deaf ear
You are God's favorite, little the doubt
The poor man, is not your peer

You have long since imploded
a black hole in the galaxy
bending the waves of light
that once emanated
from my eyes
the gravitational pull
of the mass of your being
has torn me asunder
forever eliminating
my ability to think
to reason
to feel
to love

A night birthed
by the macabre
final breath death rattles
clogging throats of the dying
indigo bats swirling en masse
plucking strands of hair
from every head uncovered
flames of torch and candle hissing
in unison with tethered serpent

brittle clank of rusted chains
shattered concrete threshholds
screams to pierce the heaven's tranquility
trailing into pleading vocal rasps

the night of the dead
with quotas to fill before dawn

priests of the unspeakable
in robed and hooded anonymity
wielding bloody daggers
oozing human sacrifice

la noche de los muertos
night of the dead....
and dying!

Now crows the death cock at first light of dawn,
salvation a lost hope, wandering in an asphalt
wilderness, heaven becomes hell.

Wailing in unknown tongues, a daylight's crier,
harbinger of evil, stumbles through deserted streets.

Scoured clean, appearing as bleached bones,
decomposed concrete harbors a foul odor.

Hairless rodents scurry in endless quest,
life sustaining spoils of war now a rarity.

Tomorrow has been canceled,

for lack of interest.

Dangling from the tattered cusp of sanity, suspended
psychosis stirs restlessly.
Amber- eyed wolves sporting gaunt bellies peer in
silence from a wooded horizon.
The voice of Legion chants in close proximity, words
foreign to the ear, disruptive to lucid thought;
featherless birds of prey circle slowly overhead.
That which was, is no more, rusted locks no longer
function; welcome to tomorrow's deserted sanctum,
welcome to liberal land, to a desolation of political
correctness.

Combat boots; old - tired
soles worn thin
Infantryman, walking
ever walking
must have walked five thousand miles
courting death
take a hill, dig in
move again
no end; never an end

short timer now, thirty more get-ups

looking good!
sniper; my name on his round
finally going home
feet first

Shame hides behind your façade, presented so
charmingly to an unsuspecting world, deceit, your
modus operandi.

You, the antithesis of good spouting words of
kindness? Ha!

To believe in you is akin to hawking seaside property
in Las Vegas, Nevada.

Grand purveyor of deception should be your formal
title, robes of black sackcloth your daily attire.

I turn my face from you as I should have done then,
before you encased me in your web.

Depart, witch! Let me die in solitude, alone in the
emptiness of your passing.

The blind are resigned to inadequate vision
quadriplegics go about the business of life
while we, the ambulatory, with eyes intact

cry out to the heavens of our misfortunes
poor souls are we, in abject self pity
begging to a benevolent deity for mercy

Lord, that we might arise from this muck
from our pitiful, introverted state of being
casting aside our Me-I attitudes, at last
reaching out with hands of help for others,
all selfishness obliterated from our minds
Becoming happily,
our brothers' and sisters' keepers.

Along the sidewalks social malfeasance festers;
unabashed derelicts lay sleeping in doorways like
rows of tiny soldiers as empty bottles stand guard.

Discarded bags that once held the prize move
aimlessly with itinerant breezes.

Stoic store fronts' benign stares through dirty window
panes bear witness.

Another corpse, stiffened in death bids farewell to the
living.

End of the line, fruition of hopelessness; agony
defined.

The ambulance leaves, its cry drowning an incessant
buzz of flies on vomit.

Discipline of self is undeniably the most necessary of human attributes; without it an individual's life can go to hell in a hurry.

We live in an era wherein self-discipline has taken a back seat to insanity, permitting all human action and interaction to become circus-like.

A child should be, and was in the recent past, disciplined under the tutelage of caring parents, learning at an early age of discipline and consequences of having a lack thereof. Now it's 'balls-to-the-wall'; screw you and screw the world, I'll do what I want when I want and you can't stop me. There is no turning from this dangerous course we are set upon. It's much like cake and ice cream at a birthday party I suppose; you can hand it out but there is no taking it back.

The world and America were better places in the past and although a majority of people will disagree with that statement, such disagreement is tied directly to a distinct absence of discipline in their own lives.

We are a snowball headed to hell as the old saying goes, and nothing can stop us now.

In throes of desperation
on the plain of nevermore,
a soul immersed in apathy
and locked outside life's door.

In tones of timid, whispered speech
the tally men (of tempest tried),
retreated from the plain post haste,
thus failed to see as spirits cried.

Away! Away! A specter's voice,
unheard but by a martyr's ear,
and spoke of such as yet unknown
for none before had ventured near.

Sleep now all infants of the dream
conceived by ghosts of yesterday,
where cherished smiles recline en masse
and not the one with words to say.

We dream, it's what we do; we hope and plan and
scheme, but above all we are dreamers.
We dream of what might be, what might have been, of
that which could be, should be and of that which can
never be.
But dreams, for the dreamer, cannot end, will not end
until one day the dreamer
becomes the dream.

Dreams tarnished
lie moldering
lonely things
deprived
youth left no warning
of intended departure
taking away hope
plundering tomorrow

aged and atrophied
bitter-sweet imaginings
languish in exile
exuberance vanquished
tears dried; dreams interred
and yet
memories linger on

Oh, heed this rambling prose my love, 'tis i have
wandered from the path
and here within this wilderness of thorn and thicket
bramble bush, life's blood will spill upon the stone
whereon i rest my head to sleep.
A dream filled night in reverie awaits, of years we
wrapped in swaddle cloth, our love, and cuddled to
the twain.

For always it was you dear girl who held me close lest
I should die, my journey from harm's way displaced
this wretched soul, baptized in joy.

A farewell sonnet now must ring in lyrics penned from
darkest blood, then scrawled across the fallen leaf
with feather borrowed from death's owl.

Remember me when thou be plagued of journey's
muddled beaten way, that somewhere now I curl a lip
in smiled salute to your goodbye.

'Twas not the fault of you alone, I was the child who'd
lost his way, and so my path is paved in pain, bonds.

Celestial trails; pathways of gods trod by beings
ethereal. Mist of the heavens, ever changing form and
direction. Beyond capacity of technology, behind
unseen vistas of wonder, universe sheathed in the
mysterious, inspiring awe among thinkers.

Who plies the seas of time across light years
inestimable, where shadowy figures dwell in solitude
and solar harmony?

Beings such as ourselves, perhaps of superior design
and construction, disdaining flesh and bone and
blood.

Of life forever, fast and free in flight, brilliant novas
proffering sustenance, indescribable pleasure in

existence, spirits riding high on the withers of Eternity.

Translucent slices of time
yesterday barely visible
images unrecognizable
shadows through fog
surreal voices moan
messages distorted
ghosts in transition
pray for guidance
spirits drifting
aimlessly

Emotions and thoughts belong neither to heart nor
mind, but to the spirit of humankind.
The spirit of man is an entity separate from all things
physical.
Do 'evil spirits' exist? Most assuredly they do as is
glaringly evident at all times and in everyplace. Yet
such spirits are not the ghosts and 'goblins' of fable
but the very essence of all human beings.
People who are evil harbor the spirit of such while evil
spirits of the dead have entered a dimension alien to
the living.
Evil spirits are devoid of that other entity called the
soul, thus their lot after death of the carrier (body)
remains a mystery. Conversely, spirits of the 'good'
are conjoined with a soul which most certainly

crosses over into a kind and gentle eternal existence
upon leaving the body which housed them during their
earthly tenure.
Should you have trouble believing any of this, keep in
mind that it is all a rambling figment of the deranged
mind of William LameBull. Cheers my friends!

Swirling, swirling nover mist,
among distorted evil sounds;
a scream heard here, a gurgle there,
in land where darkest things abound.
The flap of wings with twenty toes,
disrupts all thought of quick escape,
as boney fingers clutch and claw
hold tight and fast upon neck's nape.
Hope is not lost, but growing pale,
to ever see the light of day;
the victim chained to victims more,
a lovely maiden led away.
What be her fate, we hear the cry,
oh, pitiful that ghastly wail;
sing holy, holy, brethren here,
let angels come with fiery grail;
to quench consuming hell-bound thirst,
and pluck us from the fire that burns,
in nightmare born of every man
whose shadow lurks in servitude,
as evil, holding candles high,
denounces purity's true worth.

Woodland wonder; pure delight
rainbow pie, a la mode
cup never empty of heaven-ade
a place in step and harmony
as brotherhood flourishes
and peace is not forgotten

a quiet spot, and gentle
of butterflies and caterpillars
and bunnies, soft and cuddly
there, love-filled comforters
to ward the evening chill
and dinner always ready

lost somewhere in time
alive and well in the mind
over the next rise, perhaps
the village of Idyll sleeps
smiling; awaiting our arrival

Who wood-a thunk thet I cud of got so smart on my
own after dropin outa skool in the tent grade not me
me I thot I wud nevr lern nuthin after thet well thet go
to sho u thet skool aint evything fakt I got a gud job I
werk in kustumer servus aint thet kool I aint so dum
as my dum ol teechr thot it gud werk heer at the
landfill I meat all the kars what cum to dump I tell
them wher to go aint thet kool well all yu kid out ther

don't wurry if you don't lik skool jes drop out lik me
cuz you bet im doin real gud
Yore frind timmy

Alas, poor wretch of furrowed brow
And shoulder hunched from birth
For me, naught but the dream
Of love's sweet embrace
The lady's gentle touch
Her kiss upon this twisted visage

A prisoner, I, of ugliness
That none should look upon this face
Oh, ye lords of man's creation
Why hast thou chosen this sad soul
To bear the brunt of human shunning
Of eyes averted at my sight

For me no joy of human love
Nay, nor the companionship of kind
A life alone, in bleakness must I bear
To dwell in windowless oblivion
Until set free, my spirit soars aloft
And beauty I possess within shall shine
For all the world to see…

I love a good story of horror, and of hell,
When ghouls slink about in the dark;

Old memories well up from, God only knows where,
Of that night I slept out in the park.

Spirits were rampant, in mood shadows dancing,
Stars fell from heaven in masses;
Zombies lurked there, under park bench and swale,
Clutching firm breasts of sweet captive lasses.

Poe stepped from the trail filled of fall's fallen leaves,
The raven sat firm on his shoulder;
My pal Vincent Price with maniacal laugh,
For all of these years, seemed no older.

O, give me the nighttime, when evil abounds,
When blood, guts and gore come a' calling;
Dark poetry tickles my fancy, friends,
I trust you not find that appalling.

Smiles steeped in innocence, beamed from a child
Your dog's head laying on your lap
These, and more are the things of substance

Flowers in the spring, following a long winter
The song of birds greeting the morning sun
A beauteous sunset, its magical colors captivating

Spicy aroma of mom's fresh-baked apple pie
The crackle of fireplace logs
And the buttery taste of popped corn

Hugging a friend in need of comfort

Kissing away a child's skinned knee
Feeling the purr of an affectionate kitten

The rustle of fall leaves underfoot
Joyful laughter from lovers walking in the park
A honking of geese, flying in formation

Meaningful things… happy sights and sounds
Life's small pleasures
True substance

From the heart of the poet
Shattered by love
Disillusioned by the lady's charm
Sailed upon an iceberg sea

He quotes another poet's words:

"For all sad words of tongue and pen,
The saddest are these, it might have been"

And so this lonely poet weeps
Upon the parchment as he pens
Words his lost love spoke to him
As she walked out the door

"Goodbye; farewell… it's over now
Please do not speak my name again;
Just let it go, as bad love does,
Sometimes you lose, sometimes you win."

Where hordes of hell in devils garb
Dance sprightly on a molten sea;
Spiders at the spinning wheel,
Angels bound by webs of woven wonder,
Bind now sweet roses, gone to ash.

Ah, then it's over, through,
My race be run for naught,
A simple cloud of dust to mark the way,
I follow fast into the moonlit night.

Bright night of starry wonder spills,
Across my way and o'er this path
Which leads me, oh, I know not where,
And yet in promise to myself
I struggle forth, that as I lose a race
Within my heart I claim the winners crown.

Fear not the darkened void
Where whispered bone and feathered wing
Gather at the feet of doom
Kneeling, praying, crying souls
Where every form of light be quelled

43

Away above the mortal plane
Grand chariots stand in readiness
To whisk away all wounded gravely
Warriors of the battle bold

Hallelujah! Comes the cry
From out the bitterness of defeat
Fear swept away by angel brooms
Evil holds no power over resolute belief

Believe!

Plying the seas of paradise
our leaky craft bears forth
seeking a fabled treasure
reputed to be far north

across the straits of honeydew
over the melon way
beyond the butterfly mountains
where frogs and fairies play

clouds of cottony candy
milk chocolate frothy waves
obstacles to overcome
in the peanut brittle caves

monsters making cherry pies
animals speaking French
dogs and kitty cats frolicking

atop an old park bench

perhaps we've found the treasure
in things we each possess
friends, family and plenty of love
are the greatest treasures, I guess

Hidden beneath indigo folds
within dank chambers of thy heart
old secrets sworn and bound in chain
of hammered hell-hot molten links
lie whimpering for swift demise
thou surely be the vixen told in tale
ensnaring even now man's soul
yet here beside thy bosom's warmth
a chill as though of death's cold grasp
slides mercilessly along the spine
where shallow drumming in this chest
belies hot blood that pumpeth there
thy crimson lips thou proffer now
nay, not a man who dare resist
then fall into thy open pit of waiting hell
there crumple like the flame singed moth
and evermore proclaim thy wonder

Would that cupid's arrow
dipped in love's miraculous potion
had found its way into
the frozen wasteland
of your heart
when spring was young
and all the world shone
of precious golden amber

immersed
in stagnation of the soul
consumed
of bitter emerald bile
self adoration became
your pursuit of choice
forsaking all others
including
me

Thinking to find a cheerful smile,
I looked upon each face of passersby.
As darkened orbs of harbored hell,
devoid of joy, baleful countenances
loomed as moody harbingers,
along the walk of every street.
Where has the joy of ether days,
in robe of brightest rainbow hues
departed to, in seeming haste?
None but the very purest young
of shining face and cherub cheek,
may lighten hearts and burdens,
casting care away and down;

that nevermore, be seen a frown!

Snow's fixin' t' fly tonight, clouds look like curdled milk, all moody, hangin' up there in a soggy mess, shades 'o soot dribbled gray sorta grinnin' down evil like.

Temperature dropped a bit, fingers are beggin' fer mittens; can't recall where I put 'em; ain't wore 'em in months.

Snow shovel's ready 't go, leanin' at the back door where it looked pretty lonesome all summer.

Yard's picked up of rakes 'n such, last 'o the tomatoes froze 't death along with the flower beds.

Ice has took hold 'o the dog's water bowl, pellet stove has replaced a chore; no more wood choppin' now.

Weather fella says 12 inches tonight, don't know how they figure that; inside information I reckon.

Well, y'all bundle up now, hear!

Leaves droop today; somber, dejected.

Massive grey clouds rejoice,
filled with torrential dampness,
smiling upon soggy friends below.

In the mists of the rain comes beauty,
swirling in upon colorful wings.

Evening grosbeaks have arrived,
their feeders filled to capacity.

God's feathered creation, a joy to behold;
wondrous winged marvels in flight,
bright orange, white, yellow and black,
a chirping kaleidoscope in motion.

Lord grant that birds shall ever be,
alive and well, for all to see!

Vertical spires of green
resembling ancient warriors
massed for battle
the slender alders
stretch ever upward
moonlight filtered
through occasional dark clouds
imparts an eeriness
to the early evening landscape

on velvet-soft wings
the great grey owl glides silently

through a magical forest
the owl's name is Death
known well to denizens
of the woodland

in tangled maze of alder
and underbrush
a kangaroo rat scurries
nocturnal drama unfolding

surgical talons grasp the prey
the furry young rat
unaware of its expiration date
never looked up

Society
has pretty much
deferred compassion
and understanding
opting instead for indifference
and apathy

we all have our 'stories'
but who cares to hear them?
Bob, the bartender?
perhaps
but how about you?

have you
offered someone cheer today?
have you

lent a helping hand to someone?
do you really care about the helpless,
hopeless and infirm?
have you made an effort
to understand the other person's views?

I'd like to believe that your answer
is in the affirmative
for we are all
in this thing called life
together

Some folks who share this tired old world with the
rest of us simply have their wrappers on a little too
tight.

These sad souls were either born with, or somehow
inherited a sorry disorder which elevated their egos to
a conspicuously high plateau. While we at street level
go about the business of doing the best we can with
our lives, an upper echelon minority looks down upon
us from the penthouses of their respective ivory
towers.

There is nothing we can do to please them, our every
effort (in their eyes) is flawed and unacceptable. We
are unable to function properly in our various lines of
employment, our opinions are the fodder of fools, and
we should really be seen and not heard.

These self-important legends-in-their-own-minds types are truly a case to be reckoned with. Everyone but them is out of step, wreaking havoc with their mental parade. How sad it must be to feel so superior to your fellow man or woman. How lonely at the mountain's peak, when night falls and you sleep alone, comforted only by your imaginings of grandeur.

I cannot begin to express to you the perfect joy of being 'low class'. Indigestion is not my arch nemesis, and I sleep soundly throughout the night. My days consist of kind words and smiles, and I listen attentively to the viewpoints of others.

In summation, the elite among us might do well to reconsider their holier-than- thou mentality, yet I find that possibility to be negatively suspect. Thus shall you and I bumble mindlessly along, simple peasants in a simple existence, giving credence to such as is supposed by our su-peer-iors.

Passion knows not of love's parameters
smoke filmed alleyway windows stare
from confined swelter of summer's heat
flophouse reeks of stale perspiration
half-lit neon offers sporadic illumination
unclothed bodies writhe in guttural concert
passion flickers in the night, then ebbs

dejected silence wafts through broken glass
acrid smoke from a cigarettes red glow
illicit nighttime rendezvous played out

She always spoke in nuance, a language I had never
learned.
Her every word, each sentence, chameleon-like;
puzzling.
'I love you', very often meant, 'Buy me something
expensive', while, 'I have a headache', was just her
little way of saying, 'Another sugar daddy's coming
over tonight; get lost, chump!'
Where had I gone wrong; taken the wrong path;
involved myself with the bitch, and bitch she was, with
a capital 'B'.
She had seemed so innocent when I first met her,
crying at a bus stop, no money for the fare. Fumbling
like a schoolboy I had forked over a twenty, chiding
her for having left home without her purse. From that
day forward I had been 'forking it over' to the point of
near bankruptcy.
Retrospect is a self adhering pin cushion, finding
great pleasure in attaching itself to the soul. At the
time however, 'naivety' was worn on my shirt sleeve,
and 'willing victim' written across my forehead. Thus
as her naïve, willing victim I had become just another
sinking vessel, capsized in the turbulent wake of her
passing.
I attended the funeral today. Last week's 'sugar-
daddy' had been a real gentleman, for his execution
of sweet Suzanne had been quick and relatively
painless. Hers was apparently not the first of several
serial type killings the guy had committed.

Suzanne must have died quite puzzled at the why of her impending demise. She had always been completely honest with her 'clientele', she thought; certainly I would have disagreed with that assessment of her past behavior.

Approaching a city bus stop as I left the cemetery, I noticed a pretty, skimpily dressed young woman seated on a bench, crying large, very wet tears. Her beautiful blue eyes pleaded silently for my help. I broke into a jog, then a full-out sprint, never once looking back.

Would that you loved me more, not less,
for I the more loved you;
and would ye now the gold ring keep,
I gave when you were true?

Before tall, dark and handsome,
slipped in on midnight's watch;
to steal away our wedding vows,
and soil love with his blotch.

Keep thee the ring, still now thy voice,
forsaken fool your pardon begs;
and leave as dust beneath your feet,
a broken heart's remaining dregs.

Across yon swale, a lovely rainbow seems to end;
which grew from nothing, out a rain-wet sky.
One may not but puzzle over nature's secrets;
her thunderous rumble and flash of light,
or sparkling stars that brighten midnight's cloak.
Leaves, green as though the emerald's kin,
transform into a crimson, golden, fall delight.
Ice, born first as flowing stream, a marvel
to perplex and tax the mind. Questions.
Where went last summer, gone once more,
as have the springs of eons past, and winters too.
Why earth rotates, why day or night or snow.
Why nothing lives forever;
I think we cannot know!

Where do you turn
when it's all gone to hell
with no one in your corner
when you're dealt a losing hand
and your luck has run out
usually two options
present themselves…
your dog
or your mother
both friends in time of need
oh, to be sure

neither can save you financially…
neither can patch up
a bad romance
but they both love you
unconditionally
which is more than you can say
for the rest
of the world

Skies drip venom
where ochre-toned clouds
convulse in throes of death
an evil stench emanates
from water and stone
where has the pathway gone
abandoned by all but the few
obliterated by sullen winds
a lizard seen scurrying here
a hairless rodent there
the serpent withdrawn and shy
children have lost their way
the dreadful spell is cast
in silent curse a melody
symphony in utter madness
inscribed upon gnawed bones
stacked in neat mounds
upon sacred ground
no longer tread
by humankind

Men and women, faces unknown
strangers along the way, seeking a smile,
a word of kindness
yet we mistrust; suspect everything
we frown, scowling ferociously
survival contingent upon suspicion
no longer safe haven, the world harbors evil
and so we are wary, maintaining safe distance
never exposing soft underbellies
new friendship declined, unjustly rejected
our shells impervious to laughter and joy
bottomless chasms surrounding us
hearts frozen
in eternal mud

Much like a peanut butter sandwich
Love sticks, and causes a choke
Washed down with a glass of milk
The next bite does the same thing

He's in the dark, a man with no clue
How can anything so seemingly nice

Push a panic button in the heart
Run! Run! As fast as you can
It's the cry of a brain now on hold

Succumbed to the smell of Chanel No. 5
Shivers induced by silky-soft hair
Eyes glazed like an iced up windshield
Words drip from a mumbled mouth;
Love? This is love? By who's definition?
He feels like his breath has been stolen

Then wedded bliss, and the 'I do' kiss
Familiarity breeds contempt, I fear
She hollers at him, and he yells back
The door slams shut as he goes for a beer
She calls her mother to cry in mom's ear
And if it's all the same to you…
I believe I'll just stay single this year!

I would die for the moment to hold you
To crush your sweet breast, oh so tight
To ravish those full crimson lips so plump
To tuck you in bed every night!

I would die for the chance to be near you
My God!, such a beautiful lass
Yes, my intentions are fully sincere
For these urges I feel will not pass!

I would die for a whiff of your heavenly skin
Just to snuggle my face to your throat

But alas, you're surrounded by bodyguards
And your home by a gator filled moat!

So I guess I'll just die; get it finished
High blood pressure comes with this lust
If you won't sneak out of the house tonight
My britches shall certainly bust!

Withering vines, bones grown brittle
stars faded in eyes once bright
body's fleshly robe diminished
youth has abandoned this place
mind once fertile lies fallow
rainbows encircle a new horizon
where wait's a wondrous cruise ship
itinerary planned; course predetermined
departures scheduled daily

Write me a love poem, darlin',
tell me sweet sugarplum lies;
whisper in words penned on paper,
some wet little kissy surprise.

Pick up that parchment and hug it,
dribble blue ink on your chest;
say that you wish I were there, dear,

to wipe all that mess from your breast.

Squeeze tight the pen that you write with,
imagine it's me in your arms;
think how my strong hands might thrill you,
as you lavished upon me your charms.

Yes, write of your love and affection,
I'll believe anything you might say;
then call me, and I'll come right over,
I've a neat little game we can play!

Whither went the prophet wise,
before I heard of pending doom;
stood he bold, but yesterday
on corner of the busy street,
proclaiming what, I cannot say
for sat I in the tavern's gloom,
drowning sorrows in stout drink;
most miserable of beings,
despised by love and life.

Then wander to a tiny room,
tears need not be concealed;
there naught but Fido shall see,
(my friend will never tell),
for friends we are until the end
when misery breathes no more,
and death has closed the final door.

Divided, even in dreams,
separate yet not,
one bccomoc many
and the many, one.
Melding over time,
forgiving trespasses,
seeking unison,
inequality thrives,
hatred enjoying
non selective application.
Philosophies flourish,
bearing gifts,
wearing ragged clothing;
sporting diamonds.
Heed thou, thy suspicions,
placing substance
before glitter;
liars are many
when truth languishes.
Remember this;
all change is not
something to be desired.

Delightful splashes of brown and gold;
green tinged edges of autumn leaves
shimmer within your beautiful eyes
as a warm and sunshiny day of fall.

Splendor should be your name,
the habitation of grace and beauty.

Gazing into wondrous spherical orbs,
a pleasure filled hypnotic experience
draws me ever inward, spellbound.

A swirling vortex propels my spirit
upward, entering through heaven's gates.

I would happily forfeit my existence,
relinquishing everything for the moment;
following you into the unknown.

Should a broken heart be my lot, let it be;
I am hopelessly captivated,
a willing prisoner, chained by infatuation,
lured through windows to your soul.

Forever is measured in goodbyes,
resounding across eons,
over corpse littered chasms
wherein broken hearts languish,
withering in pity of self.

Hell has not the fury of woman
scorned once, then set upon

a crusade of wanton revenge,
every male her chosen victim.

Flee in swiftness over broiling seas,
where agony treads water,
lurking in lust; waiting patiently
with hangman's noose in hand.

Suffering the intolerable,
(death by his own hand)
a solution despised,
yet accepted.

Life had been good
until now.

The children grown,
his wife gone before him;
it was time to leave.

She waited even now,
Somewhere,
somber at his decision
yet anxious for reunion.

His brief note told all,
not ambiguous in its finality;
"Going to see Mom.
Don't wait up for me.

Love, Dad."

Lies suspected
so long concealed
where spiders lurk
and centipedes
in anonymity
dank and dark
cerebral passageways
blocked
soiled robes
in rumpled heaps
scattered carelessly
impediments to truth

Tread ever softly and fear the dark,
your vision limited where lurkers lie in wait.
Evil intentions find ample concealment
within the folds of indigo shadows.
Screams stifled in constricted throats,
vocalization limited to ghastly gurgles
of souls who passed this way before.
What hides beyond, scant feet ahead,
or slithers even now, unseen?
Hurry - quickly, swiftly move;

stumble not on sidewalk's broken surface,
lest there you meet the ghouls that haunt;
whose wailing fills the nighttime hours,
and chills the marrow bone of all mankind.
Run! Now run, no time to tarry here,
for death astride a thing macabre
closes fast upon your heels.
RUN!, looking never back,
for should you meet the monster's eye
your fate be sealed, you surely die!

Signed in the presence of God and man,
words on parchment inscribed;
married, become man and wife this day,
and never the twain shall part
signed, sweet vows, within each heart,
emblazoned on minds and souls,
love honor and cherish, unwritten
two golden bands placed on fingers,
two voices seal heaven's contract
they, signed in marriage,
irrevocable

Death, despair and disparity. Eyes that see not, and

mouths spewing riddles. Life games played by adults who would be children; cops chased by robbers. Charlatans leading the naïve, as rats abandon sinking vessels. Where the good ship Lollypop; why the dream abandoned. Having come full circle, we chase our tails, never gaining in an ill conceived pursuit. Fabricate tales of tomorrow, laying waste the truths of the day; dig deep your pitfalls on every pathway, covering them over with sweet scented blooms. Embrace your leaders as they thrust, then twist the rusted knife blade in your heart.

What motive behind a willing grin,
When the world seems down and out;
Why, that smile amid the tears,
Why not, a sullen pout?

Words of encouragement spewing,
Out from the mouth of defeat;
Comes laughter without reason,
From a spirit, can never be beat.

Laugh and the world will follow,
Speak words of endearment this day;
Offer your hand to a stranger,
Found fallen along the way.

Joy be your constant companion,
Giving, your code and your creed;
Toss out all conflict and worry,
Think outside your own selfish need.

You may not think love is life's answer,
Yet love is a place we can start;
Love one another while loving yourself,
Let love's rainbow shine from your heart.

Possessing little more than memories,
the old man sat rocking in a battered chair on the porch.

His frame, obviously that of a once strong
and muscular individual appeared frail now.

He stared straight ahead, his gaze unflinching.

It was the look of the front line combat veteran.

It's called the 1000 yard stare, a characteristic
of combat vets who, tested and tried at the enemy's doorway
have slipped a little over the edge.

The years aren't kind to any of us.

We get used up and cast aside by the times in which we live.

For a brief period, vibrant and youthful,
we find ourselves all too soon the wrinkled and forgotten citizens
of a nation uncaring, and therein gone quite mad.

In these days more than at any period in our history, the aging person is considered a detriment to society.

We suck up too many tax dollars in so-called social security,
a system which is anything but.

Shunned by the majority of our countrymen and women, we wither and die, left alone with only the memories that we dread or cherish, each in it's time.

So it was with Sam. He'd been there.
Hell yes, he'd been there; he had done it all.
The youth of this age had not an inkling of the things he'd seen and done.

None of the kids these days could have survived Sam's experiences, he was certain. Well, the times had changed. You couldn't blame these kids for the way in which they were brought up, he thought.

Everything changes; maybe that's how it should be. He was glad he'd done his time while the world was real; in an era before everything had gone to hell.
....

A nurse found the old gentlemen in his chair on the porch. He had stopped rocking, but his eyes were still fixed on something she wasn't able to see. There was a hint of a smile on his face.

Taps had beckoned the old vet, but life had been good. He was free now, and off to join his memories.

That littlo nip upon tho nooc
announces autumn's splendor;
and lightly frosted pumpkins,
their tasty pies shall render.

The trees, deciduous and grand
flaunt leaves of red and gold;
While geese in V form overhead
honk goodbyes to the cold.

Upon the ground in piles of fluff,
the maple leaves grow higher;
and in the homes along some lane
folks feed the wood stove's fire.

The hills ablaze in color, laugh,
against a sky of Prussian blue;
'tis heaven sent, this time of year,
meant just for me and you!

Disheveled streetwalker passing by
Rumpled clothing; weathered face
Beauty obviously dwelled there once
Before life's ravages intervened

Silent cry for help emanates
From fearful look on tear stained face
Not more than thirty years of age
And yet, might well be fifty-plus

Eyes pleading; quietly praying
Approaching stranger notices
Thus taken by the woman's plight
Steps out in front to block her way

A furtive look; her chapped lips part
"What would it be you want of me?"
In voice not changed by circumstance
But sounding like the angels' harps

"I've come to save you from this hell
Of living here, upon the streets"
She, spoken to within her heart
Somehow knows he speaks the truth

Angel sent from heaven; savior or saint?
A soul-mate born of fairytales, perhaps
Yet only these few words she speaks;

"Take my hand and lead me away."

Where now, that brilliant orb
of summer's gilded face,
reflects a mood of joy fulfilled
yet cannot keep the pace;
with happy spirits' unencumbered
leaping as the merry clown,
over fields in rainbow dress,
through every back place; every town;
comes festive music, on the breeze
a piper playing fantasy;
and every note from out that horn
is written just for you and me!

On the backside of never where always once lived
you spoke to me words made of silk;
kisses as warm as the hot August sun,
words tasting of honey and milk

why hast thou left me alone with my fears,
where the sweet love swilled as wine;
how have we come to this parting of ways,
when did I lose what was mine

was it something I said to offend thee;
does my breath smell of onion or worse;
are you simply a witch on a broomstick,
destroying my love with a curse

your words sound of ice in the winter,
those lovely hands freeze at my touch;
when I go to my maker, leaving this world,
even then will I love you as much

Existing in silent reticence
Mysteries of the mind
Flashed upon ancient cave walls
Dark cerebral caverns
Secrets sometimes cherished
Often despised; mentally reviled
The lie twice two times told
....
A hidden corpse now long forgot
The attic box Pandora owned
No peace for unrepentant souls
Concealing ghosts of yore
....
The mind knows well of mysteries
Which haunt and torture
Night and day
And never cease their cry

To be revealed

Memories of the coldest winter
Stark; genuine; haunting
Seventy degrees below zero
Three weeks on end it stayed
Diesel fuel gelled in copper tubing
A one inch flame burned valiantly
In the pot burner's belly
A tiny family huddled for warmth
Dressed in every available garment
Robed in pilfered bedding
Staring through the glass opening
Watching that candle -size flame
Hell is not hot my friends
The hinterlands are bathed in cold
And Satan wears parka and mukluks
We survived and are the stronger
But stronger yet is the memory
Three weeks of hell in a cabin
one lifetime of a family's bond
Chiseled into the stone of posterity

A veil of white fishnet lace
embellished with tiny white roses
conceals mysterious dark eyes

A single strand of raven-black hair
escapes from the garment
attempting to fly away
but is quickly captured

Not easily distinguishable
the lithe figure of femininity
beneath a black robe
is nonetheless begging
to be noticed

This is not my land
not my country
customs here dictate
looking away quickly

I shall sleep fitfully tonight
dreaming that I have
removed the veil
discarded the robe
and feverishly licked crimson lips

I awaken to the smell
of patchouli oil
she has come to my room

If I am beheaded tomorrow

so must it be

She was a ravishing beauty.
Me? Just the 'ugly duckling';
the kid who lived next door.
Every boy in town wanted her.
She was coy to the enth;
little sideways glances,
half smile on her lips,
eyes lowered; blink, blink.

She dated the better looking guys,
one after another.
If I was on her list ,she never quite got to my name.
My heart was crushed.
Adolescent puppy-love overwhelmed me.
I was torture for me, every time
she left her house with another guy.

She married Tommy Smarty-Pants,
the handsome, well-to-do class president,
right after graduation.
I wonder sometimes how they're doing.
I think of her once in awhile;
like every day.
Maybe it was more than puppy-love,
for after all this time,
I am still
heartbroken.

Neath a moon of a million promises,
Midst shadow and platinum light;
Lies are spewed from the devil's mouth,
"I love thee", a liar's blight…

Thou love me not, knave; only thyself,
Why takest thee liberties now ?
Plucking this heart from the breast ye have held,
And that, after showing me how…

A child of sixteen, my dear father's girl,
You've sullied and spoiled my life;
Thou leavest tomorrow to seek a new love,
And take her, perhaps, as thy wife…

You smile as though nothing here matters,
A fling in this straw of the field;
What be thy reason for hating me so ?
And that after knowing full yield…

Go then, look never behind thee,
My father shall fine gallows build;
The grave even now, sir, awaits thee;
May worms seek you out when 'tis filled !

A dusty pathway beckons,
skirting boulders and trees,
winding ever up on the mountainside.

This trail's angle of attack is steep,
rising inches to each foot gained.

The valley floor drops away as I climb,
Its gravel road becoming serpent-like,
slithering down the canyon towards town.

Small risers of dust indicate travel
yet no automobile sound emanates.

Across the valley I spot two bull elk;
I smile knowing they have seen me as well.

In my mind I yell "better hide boys"
hunters will be coming soon enough.

A golden eagle circles, watching me,
her nest perched on the cliff just above.

My quest among these treacherous boulders
Is for the giant calcite crystal, an elusive gem,
and if fortunate perhaps even the rare opal.

It is tremendously beautiful here on these cliffs,
quiet but for the occasional gentle breeze
and at times like this I imagine staying up here,
all of life's din and clutter left to a hectic world below.

Nourished, groomed
for many years
the bonsai grew
and thrived

the caregiver
of the little tree
aged as do men
the tree, as a tree

the bonsai now 100
the caretaker dead
at 90
disparity

Lilies stand across the field, from hither o'er to yon,
Between the crosses of the brave, where dog tags
hang thereon;

They, young and eager went to fight an enemy
unknown,
Faceless soldiers in the fray, who never did come
home;

Battles fought for cause unclear, each told the war
was right,
The cries of wives and mothers too, now echo
through the night;

Across an ocean, lonely graves in somber silence
speak,

Ten thousand spirit voices cry, 'ken ye' what war doth wreak?'

There, not one soul who for his country would not go again,

How sweet will turn to sour
and ne
that everything was good

the face turned slightly
avoiding any eye contact
lips taking on a winter chill
arms now unwilling to hold

when did love
fly out the window
on wings of an errant wind
as hope yet flourished
within a fools heart

one remains silent
one weeps in silence
while questions
beg in vain

Where have you been little one
'neath bush and stone a' hiding
the sun so warm upon thy skin
in shade thou were abiding
in bramble thicket dense and deep
thy brothers lie a' waiting
to venture out upon the plain
the temperatures abating
soft furry coat thou wearest now
clean licked is sure a' shining
the sun begins it's fast descent
'tis nearly time for dining
feathers ruffle there above
eyes narrowed at the sound
a gleam of whetted canines
thou melt into the ground
a flying leap, extended claw
thy brothers aid the tether
upon a black and shiny nose
a single downy feather

Dark things scurry into crevices
the mind tortured; twisted
visions convulse
writhing in agony
where indigo vultures circle
screams; cries
agonized whimpers
emanate from lips
scoured by brimstone

stretched tightly
across yellowed teeth
painful grimaces
grotesque painting
reality or fantasy
dream
or death

Swilling from his cup of brew, he sat upon the river's bank and forthwith threw his baited hook into the listless current.

The tiny fire he'd built for cheer more than warmth exuded it's intended bits of pleasure in the crackle of burning wood, and in flames of yellow-orange hue.

The odor of smoke was an old friend, a delight to fishermen everywhere, and the occasional burning of eyes or tickled nostrils only added to the moment... one of life's genuine pleasures.

His fishing rod, weathered through many seasons of use was propped in the fork of a willow Branch, freshly cut for the occasion, and planted in the soft ground.

A fat trout jumped, barely clearing the water's surface, nabbing a winged insect then disappearing, leaving only concentric rings upon the water to mark its airborne debut.

The fisherman smiled, at peace with himself; in harmony with the universe... wondering that man must become old before appreciating the small things... life's true pleasures.

...

Hours later, newly arrived fishermen approached the old gentleman's fishing spot, where he leaned in repose against the backrest of a small tree stump, his fire burned out and his eyes closed.

His line was jerking wildly... a nice fish had taken the bait but the old fisherman was unaware.

As the new arrivals stood over the reclining fellow his passing became apparent.
The man, in death, was the quintessence of a life fully lived... truly appreciated.
Those standing there marveled at the smile affixed upon the old man's face.

One of the fishermen picked up the old gentleman's fishing pole and began retrieving his catch. "It's a nice one, Pop", the man said.

Rickety old bones in rickety old bodies, traversing the ragged and precipitous slopes of life are too soon lost amid the broken shards and rubble of years.
As wisps of expelled breath, brief moments in the sun are lost to space and time. How can it be, where lies an answer to perplexing questions mouthed but never spoken?
Why did not the thunder cease nor the rain stop for

our parade? Where have these wrinkles come from, they that replaced this once firm and vibrant skin? Yesterday must surely have been a figment, an apparition, a dream, dreamed while we were yet awake. Tomorrow's aging profile, unannounced, proffers even now its impending arrival, solidifying suspicions of youth recently departed.
Time so brief, so perilous and as we cruise through season upon ever changing season we are want to ignore the signs of our own season of change. Nothing endures the rigors of time, not even the elements of earth and moon and stars.
We enter life as fragile creatures and in the fragility known to age we succumb to human mortality. No living human knows what lies beyond the grave, not even those who believe that they have made that journey through so-called near death experiences. Acknowledge age as it eats away at your youth and vigor. Make peace with it for truly there exists no option.

On bareback pony she arrives,
racing over straw-brown fields,
raven hair trailing in the wind,
Flower's petals loosed, to fly away,
abandoning her tangled locks.

As now beside the pony comes,
running silently along its flank,

a lone gray wolf, magnificent.

A vision born of fantasy,
yet I would pray that it be real,
the huntress seeking hard my heart,
as I, her willing prey await.

Then borne away to paradise,
upon that wondrous pony's back,
my arms encircle naked breasts,
her hair perfumed of wild musk
infiltrates nostrils, and I shout

'Tis drunk I am, intoxicated,
lost in storybook romance;
awake me not here as I dream,
of love idyllic evermore.

Barney was born in the backseat
Mom was a two-bit whore
Dad was somebody nobody knew
And rotten to the core

Mom's name was Ruby Spencer
Barney, a bastard at birth
Grew up on his own full of hatred
On the streets of a gulf coast firth

Fighting and thievery his forte
Barney learned everything well
The devil, both mother and father

His hometown the hot streets of hell

One night Barney shot a policeman
Killed him right there on the spot
Ran for three months to the very day
When surrounded, Barney was caught

Not his fault he was born a bastard
Going bad was the choice he made
The decider makes the decisions
For whatever foundation is laid

All you "Barneys" who turn to evil
You make your own bed, so they say
Crawl into bed with the devil
And that's where you're going to lay!

Taken over by weeds
it's weathered wooden marker leaning
precariously
the cross's horizontal bar
points either up
or down
depending upon the perspective
of the viewer

this long forgotten place
home to rabbits and birds
lizards, mice
and snakes
houses much more

beneath the sun parched surface
remains of one who knew the world
before us
lies in repose
dust now
the spirit long ago released

no name is legible
on gnarled silver wood
i wonder who you are
what you did
who you loved and laughed with
where you are now

Sasquatch, Bigfoot, Bushman, Yeti
Abominable Snowman...
Aliens, Spaceships and
weird abductions

Overactive imagination
Paranormal, psychics
Witchcraft
Ooohhh!

A lifetime in the outdoors
The nighttime sky
And wild places
Revealing nothing

Ghosts avoid my presence
As though I were

A scary thing
Ooohhh!

Why are so many privy
To the unseen
While I wait
In vain

Within the forest's fence of trees
Where fairy beings flit and fly
Imagined moments playing there
Are captured in a youngster's eye

In house of roots beneath a floor
Of fallen leaves and twiggy stem
The children dance on thistledown
As fairy fiddlers play for them

When evening settles o'er the wood
And fireflies their lanterns light
Imaginary little folks
All gather 'round to say goodnight

Then sleeping peaceful in their beds
The children dream of fun and play
As once again the forest calls
"Come little ones, it's time to play"!

In the trenches of time
Love and hate, and beauty
Alongside loneliness, despair
And all things ugly
Lie awaiting burial

This mass gravesite
The place where all things
Become meaningless
As they will be now
As they should have been
In life

Yesterday and years forgotten
Harbingers of today,
Tomorrow, and things
Not yet encountered
Meaningless
Devoid of substance
Tears, long dried

Truth rings like tiny tinker bells
when whispered in the ear of love
melodious and charming
and knows the moment
oh so well

Enveloped now in headiness

words warmly wrapped
in swaddling cloth
perfume thy cheek
this captive soul caress

Silken shrouds of lovely hair
anoint, then steal the breath away
willing prisoner, this smitten heart
shall live in bondage
evermore

White thistledown, o'er fields blown
by summer's breath, reeking of sunshine,
where painted butterflies in shades
of vibrant colors, drawn from nature's rainbow palette,
dance upon the flowers' heads,
coating themselves in golden nectar

there, lizards scurry, hurry… wait,
for insects lost to moments thought…. then caught!

a bird in feathers tinged with red, sings…
monotonous trill drowning the buzz
of busy honey bees… whose efforts never cease

tail's twitch discloses deer, camouflaged
under foliage shrouded branches
drooping to the ground

this place is sacred
for man has not yet covered it

in asphalt

'Tis not the day I dread nor shine
Of sun upon my face, old friend,
It is the night when vultures wait
To feast upon me at the end

Oh God of heaven, spare my soul
When all my bones lay white,
Each morsel plucked and eaten
As the worms give up the fight

Dust is to dust this flesh no more
The wayward spirit since set free,
To drift about the universe
And settle where, no man agree

The dead care not of fruited plain
Not hunger, thirst or wanting,
The ghosts of all who ever pass
Are simply bent on haunting

Let no man sleep without full measure
Spent upon the toils of living,
After life on earth be done
Trust God shall keep on giving

Tthere exists no window in time
the past lies buried

in fields of forgotten dreams
that which the future may hold
has yet to be born
the panes of glass
we might have looked through
stand silent in muddied obedience
to incongruity
whoever shall greet the future's arrival
will see it then
while those who wait
for a glimpse of the past
will surely miss the bus

Beer joint some call it; to others a tavern
small dark interior where bluish cigarette smoke
drifts aimlessly, its segregated layers
gently descending; hovering over patrons
whose faces bear agonies unspoken

sad people, laughing to mask the pain
of a hundred sorrows
drinking; hoping memories will disappear
stumbling finally into taxicabs or alleyways
some returning to empty apartments
without friend or family

not all are derelicts
some even affluent

yet beneath the surface
under the guise of cheer
the same story
pathetic
sad
people

Borne upon solar winds of eternity
I have caressed the breasts of time,
fondling her celestial gems,
drifting down galactic rivers of pleasure,
her rapids an intoxicating rush;
a vortex of swirling planetary pools.

Adrift upon a sea of salvation
the intrepid lady Time takes my hand,
freeing me of earthly bondage;
loosed to fly with her among angels.

Never was a 'hunk' type; didn't chase girls…stayed
away from 'em.
Hell, country boy raised in poverty, no car, ragged-ass
clothes….and then we relocated to a city. Ugh!
Whole new ballgame. Had t' wear shoes to school for
one thing; shucks, even started combing my hair.
It was hard catchin' on to city ways. Time was we got

to go into town for one movie a year; now we started going to the old Rialto theatre every weekend. Price of admission at a couple theatres was a nickel, but the Rialto cost 9 cents. Man, did I get into those old shoot-em-ups.

Anyway, back to the girl thing; I preferred hunting and fishing or even just trampin' through the woods t' getting' cozy with girls. Shoot, they all scared the dickens outa me. Now, these many years later I know why that was.

Finally took a girl out on my first date. Man, she was all perfumed up n' had on the softest feelin' cweater I'd ever felt. Went to a movie…gradually slipped an arm around her shoulders. She gets all uppity and says, "Your arm is really uncomfortable."

Well, that did it; I gave up on girls for another few years. Hound dogs n' fishin' poles never talked back or got persnickety like that gal did. Got out of the army on my first hitch in '55. Dated a time or two but always with the wrong girl it seemed. Hell, I ain't doubting for a minute that I was a real dud. I reenlisted in '56 and kept my mind on military matters instead of women. Then in late '59 I met a real gem (yeah, right!) and married her. Damn, I should have stayed in the army….getting' shot at beats bein' hollered at 24-7. Now here I am, old (used but not used up), one foot in the grave and the other slippin' on a damned banana peel, married to a little darlin' named AnnaBeth and she tolerates me pretty well. We're different as day n' night in a lot o' things, but I finally figured out that there are still a few good gals out there in La-La land.

Silken tresses
sun burnished
glitter as gold
in a clear mountain stream
Aphrodite reincarnate
descending from heaven
she envelops my senses
and we elope, entwined
upon her magical carpet
sipping aphrodisiac of gods
plying celestial seas
making love
exploring one another
exploring the universe
uninhibited

Had a flat one night, many years ago. Dark and
dreary; raining cats and dogs. No spare tire.
A car pulled up behind myself and two friends in our
old '49 ford.
Fella exits his car and approaches the driver's side
window. I roll the glass down; "You boys having
problems?"
"Yes sir. Flat tire and no spare."
The guy goes to his car, removes a jack, comes back,
takes off the flat tire, throws it in his car and leaves.
Strange.
Forty five minutes later he's back with a repaired tire.
He puts it on our car, removes the jack, gets back in
his car and is gone before we can ask who, why, what
or even say thank you.

I still ask myself after all these years, was that an angel...an apparition, or just a good Samaritan?

I've always loved you
and yet
I have never
understood you.

An indisputable anomaly
you were swept into my life
by an ill wind,
taking me
hostage.

A prisoner
of indefinable charm,
I wear unseen shackles
which have cut deeply
into this captive spirit.

O, to have realized
long before your arrival
the utter hopelessness
of this incompatibility.

Perhaps one day
the wind which brought you
shall once again
come this way,
whisking you
from my life.

If you've never spit in the devil's eye
Or thumbed your nose at hell
If you knuckle down to another's demands
And jump when they ring the bell

If you whimper alone in darkness
Beneath covers where none may see
And don a façade in daylight
While praying to be set free

Then you my friend are a faker
Telling lies you've come to believe
You might just as well cry out to the stars
In that silent place where you grieve

Pull your head from the sand that blinds you
Grab those bootstraps and give a hard yank
Freedom is worth more than what you possess
You can take this advice to the bank!

Dearest heart, why cometh thee now,
bearing in arms the fruit of our love,
when thou hast long forsaken that love?

Yea, the boy child be of my own blood
and care for him I surely shall do,
but nay, never shall we two join as one.

With my own brother didst thou lie down,
as I laboured in diligence for this family.

Thy shame has besmirched us all,
a grievous insult to our love inflicted by thee,
an adulteress, no better than a harlot.

Here then, take this purse of coin and go;
depart my presence, never to return
for to look upon your face again I cannot bear.

Hatred, dislike and dissention,
stomachs in acidic turmoil,
signs of the times perhaps,
life's potential diminished.

Cerebral inadequacies abound,
ill conceived feelings; bad vibes
fostered and nourished by fools
steeped in the devil's sour elixir.

What cost to the individual,
his or her caring and compassion;
understanding and tolerance,
and a fair amount of patience?

Be at peace with yourself through
extending acceptance to others,
remembering always the admonition,
"Do unto others as you would have them
do unto you…"

Ah Poe, now lieth thee
in place of soggy molded earth
when to the pyre thou might have gone,
ashes melding with earth's spirit force.

Why the grave, a dark and lonely hole
where sunshine never rears its head
nor doth a silver moonbeam light the way.

I choose the crematory's flame,
that all consuming fire igniting flesh and bone,
that never shall this spirit be confined,
rather set loose to fly upon celestial winds
thus cavorting with my own.....forever free!

Of love I sang so long ago
and as I mouthed each sweet refrain
came from the clouds an evil rain
to sweep away my every joy
to steal from me my heart
Of love I sang, 'neath glorious skies
the lyrics rang to heaven's skirts

but O', how desolation hurts
when love has taken leave and fled
Of love I sang, but sing no more
an angel called my love away
destroyed the dream, I've lost my way
now ever shall I wander
alone

Her castle sports no marble halls;
bandana 'round her forehead,
she cleans the kitchen floors.
Preparing yet another evening meal,
remembering back to when they met;
love had blown in from nowhere,
settling firmly upon her heart.
Her hand he'd asked, in marriage;
with anticipation's breath,
she whispered yes, oh yes!
The children now have flown the nest,
yet love has never faded.
The front door opens;
he is home from work,
the only man she's ever loved.
In warm embrace they stand;
the kiss, the touch, the moment,
and with the same breath of anticipation
they speak in unison;
"I love you!"

Not the grave for this bag of bones,
a funeral pyre, stoked high;
nobody's planting my butt in the ground,
and damn them to hell should they try!

Worms live in the sod, and little more,
grubs and ants, where water seeps;
a dark and dank and dreary place,
just imagining gives me the creeps!

Off to Valhalla, to heaven or hell,
not a single farewell as I go;
grinning from out my ashes when spread,
when they fall to the gardener's hoe!

Buttermilk whispers, sweet to the ear,
conjuring mental images, visions,
imaginings of bodies entwined
as when love was fresh and new.
Buttermilk whispers, curdled now,
unfit for the heart's consumption,
left beside a dumpster
for removal.

It lurks in darkness, a thing of beauty

Entrapped by design, a prisoner in waiting.
A formidable opponent of things thyroidal,
it waits patiently in wraps, seeking release,
soft, svelte, master of enticement it is,
a purveyor of longing, whispering promises.
It owns no conscience, ever calling out
to the minds of the weak and gullible,
to the unwary who drool at its mention.
Beware the dreaded beast, chocolate!
gooey, chewy, dark and yummy,
a delectable delight...out to get you!

Tough, weathered riders in love with the wind
Chasing a lost asphalt dream
Utopia smiling around the next bend
In a valley of honey and cream

In leathers worn shiny from years on the road
With eyes that stare right through your face
Their world growing small; their time has grown thin
The old bikers are losing the race

It's a race to catch freedom before it escapes
A dash to find something at all
Intrinsic; unknown; a voice in their heads
Just a dream of some good place to fall

But the riders rode high on the withers of time
In their youth they were masters and kings
How ghastly the ravage of time on a man

How despised the change that it brings

With muscles in atrophy; rhino skin faces
Hands growing weaker each year
The body rebels at the bumps in the road
And they've hiked up the price of a beer

Oh the world's gone to hell and we know it
We're just riding along in its wake
Setting the pace for a new breed
Who ride bikes that cost more than we make

But the memories we have and take with us
Of our time in a place you won't ken
Beat the hell out of modern time T-shirts
Telling all of the world where you've been

Crack the throttle boys hear the wind rushing
See that sunrise coming over the hill
Valhalla lies just 'round that bend in the road
And we'll meet there, damned sure we will

Growin' up dirt poor has its advantages. For one
thing, bad guys can't steal what you don't have.
I never knew until I went into the army that I couldn't
see for shit. Got a couple pair of glasses then and
saw my first ever dentist.
My immediate and extended families all survived on
the same food stuff. We hunted moose and caribou,
ate potatoes (boiled, fried, baked and a few other
ways) and almost always smothered in gravy made

from flour and water in the same fryin' pan the
venison was fried in. Mornings were either oatmeal or
sourdough hotcakes and we caught plenty of salmon,
killed spruce hens and ptarmigan and figured pretty
much that we were wealthy. Good stuff, that sorta
food. Love it to this day, although haven't tasted any
in years.
It's a shame that the 'poor' of today can't survive as
we did back then, but it's hard t' find the critters we
ate a' strollin' down the urban streets of America. Too
bad; the homeless wouldn't have t' do any damn
dumpster divin' to get by. Just thinkin' out loud I
reckon. Have a nice evening.

Blessed be thy pouty lips,
those petulant, pleasurable orbs
for these do I adore.
Blessed be the warm embrace
which I have come to covet.
Blessed be thy love, dear girl
which thou giveth freely.....

The defeated spirit
hoes a hard row,
derelicts of old skid row
where seedy taverns dot

a pathetic landscape,
where hope long ago
retreated in disgust.
Lonely this lot of rag tags
bent on self destruction
hardened hearts, mottled livers,
existing for the next score,
that final bottle.

Should I not love thee the more,
that your father is a man of wealth?
Could I, the poor goat herder
become his doting son-in-law,
sharing his hollow mirth;
coddling and admiring
while feigning affection?

What worth, a love true and righteous,
taken at value of face,
with strings attached thereto;
a pure and simple love, and enduring?

But lo, thy father disliketh me
for reason undisclosed;
mayhap my handsome countenance
illuminates his own hawkish features.

Wouldst thou, then, elope with me,
clinging to my loins, astride a valiant winged steed,
while racing through the nighttime wood;
a forest bathed of full moon glow?

Come, the time be now to leave thy nest,
for fear thy father's henchmen rise,
to forever quell this heart which beats
within the cavern of love's abode.

Up; away to run upon a moonbeam's wings,
across the universe, we two, in joyous harmony,
to wed upon a sea of stars,
our marriage of heaven's making,
baptized in holiness - sanctified by angels;
when you and I are we, my love;
when you and I are we...

Thank you for reading my little book of scribbles!

William "Frenchy" DeRushe-LameBull

Made in the USA
San Bernardino, CA
06 February 2018